Uranus

by Gregory L. Vogt

Consultant:
Ralph Winrich
Aerospace Education Specialist
for NASA

Bridgestone Books
an imprint of Capstone Press
Mankato, Minnesota

Bridgestone Books are published by Capstone Press
151 Good Counsel Drive, P.O. Box 669, Mankato, Minnesota 56002
http://www.capstone-press.com

Library of Congress Cataloging-in-Publication Data
Vogt, Gregory.
    Uranus/by Gregory L. Vogt.
    p. cm.—(The galaxy)
    Includes bibliographical references and index.
    Summary: Discusses the surface features, atmosphere, orbit, moons, rings, and
exploration of the planet Uranus.
    ISBN 0-7368-0517-6
    1. Uranus (Planet)—Juvenile literature. [1. Uranus (Planet)] I. Title. II. Series.
QB681.V64 2000
523.47—dc21
                                                                            99-046832
                                                                                  CIP

Editorial Credits

Tom Adamson, editor; Timothy Halldin, cover designer and illustrator; Kimberly Danger
    and Jodi Theisen, photo researchers

Photo Credits

Astronomical Society of the Pacific/NASA, 16
Courtesy of NASA/JPL/Caltech, 6
Erich Karkoschka (University of Arizona) and NASA, 16 (inset)
NASA, cover, 1, 8, 10, 12, 14, 18 (all), 20

1 2 3 4 5 6 05 04 03 02 01 00

Table of Contents

Relative size of the Sun and the planets

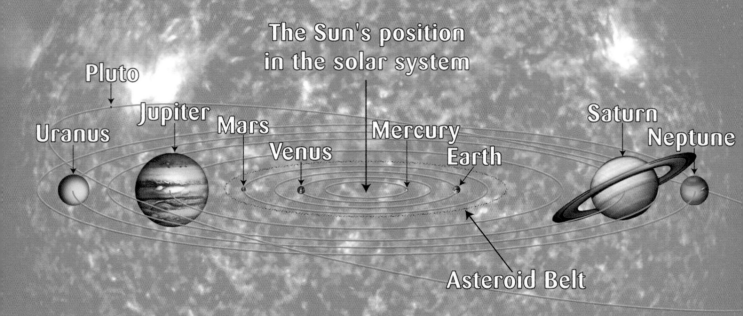

Pluto

Jupiter

Uranus

Mars

Venus

The Sun's position
in the solar system

Mercury

Earth

Saturn

Neptune

Asteroid Belt

The Sun

Uranus is a planet in the solar system. The Sun is the center of the solar system. Planets, asteroids, and comets travel around the Sun.

Uranus is one of the giant outer planets made of gases. Jupiter, Saturn, and Neptune are the other outer planets. Four rocky inner planets are closer to the Sun. Mercury, Venus, Earth, and Mars are much smaller than the outer planets. Pluto is the farthest planet from the Sun. Pluto is small and is made of rock and ice.

Uranus does not receive as much light and heat from the Sun as Earth does. Life as we know it could not survive on Uranus.

◄ **This illustration compares the sizes of the planets and the Sun. Uranus is the third largest of the giant gas planets. The blue lines show the orbits of the planets. Thousands of asteroids move around the Sun. The asteroid belt is between the orbits of Mars and Jupiter.**

FAST FACTS

	Uranus	Earth
Diameter:	31,764 miles (51,118 kilometers)	7,927 miles (12,756 kilometers)
Average distance from the Sun:	1,784 million miles (2,871 million kilometers)	93 million miles (150 million kilometers)
Revolution period:	84 years	365 days, 6 hours
Rotation period:	17 hours, 14 minutes	23 hours, 56 minutes
Moons:	at least 18	1

The Planet Uranus

Uranus is the third largest planet in the solar system. Uranus is 31,764 miles (51,118 kilometers) wide. The planet is four times wider than Earth.

Uranus is the seventh planet from the Sun. It is about 1,784 million miles (2,871 million kilometers) from the Sun. People can see Uranus only on a very clear night away from city lights. Through a telescope, Uranus looks like a small blue-green disk.

William Herschel discovered Uranus in 1781. Herschel was a British musician. Astronomy was his hobby. He saw Uranus through a telescope he had built.

Herschel wanted to name the planet after King George III of England. But all planets except Earth are named for Greek and Roman gods. Later astronomers named the planet Uranus after the Greek god of the sky.

This image shows Uranus and the five largest of its 18 moons.

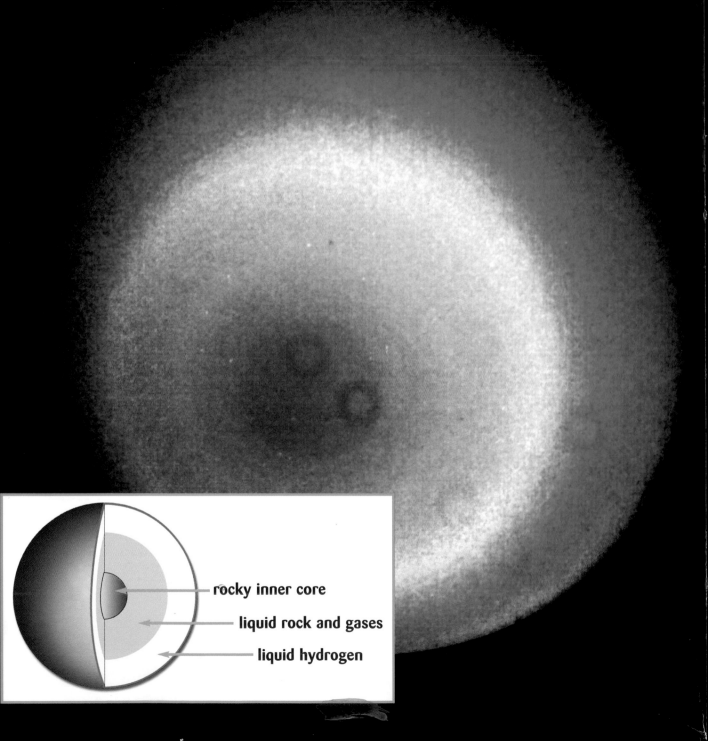

rocky inner core

liquid rock and gases

liquid hydrogen

The Atmosphere of Uranus

Like the other giant gas planets, Uranus does not have a solid surface. Instead, Uranus has a thick atmosphere. This mixture of gases forms a layer around a planet. Uranus's atmosphere is made up of hydrogen and helium gases. Its atmosphere also has small amounts of methane and acetylene gases. Methane in the upper atmosphere gives Uranus its blue-green color.

The upper atmosphere of Uranus is cloudy. Strong winds blow the clouds around the planet at speeds of up to 650 miles (1,050 kilometers) per hour. The clouds keep astronomers from seeing more of the planet. The temperature in the upper atmosphere is about minus 350 degrees Fahrenheit (minus 210 degrees Celsius).

Scientists discovered a layer of smog near the south pole of Uranus. Sunlight heats the gases in this area. The heat makes the gases look like smog.

The colors in this picture show an area of smog at Uranus's south pole.

Uranus lies on its side as it rotates.

Like all planets in the solar system, Uranus revolves around the Sun. Planets follow a path called an orbit as they move around the Sun. Earth makes one revolution around the Sun every year. Uranus is farther from the Sun. Uranus takes 84 years to make one trip around the Sun.

Uranus also rotates, or spins, while it orbits. The planet rotates once every 17 hours and 14 minutes. Unlike most planets, Uranus lies on its side as it rotates. For part of Uranus's orbit, its north pole points toward the Sun. Forty-two years later, the planet's south pole points toward the Sun.

William Herschel wanted to name the planet he discovered "Georgium Sidus," or "King George's Star," after King George III. Later astronomers named the planet Uranus after the Greek god of the sky. This symbol stands for the planet Uranus.

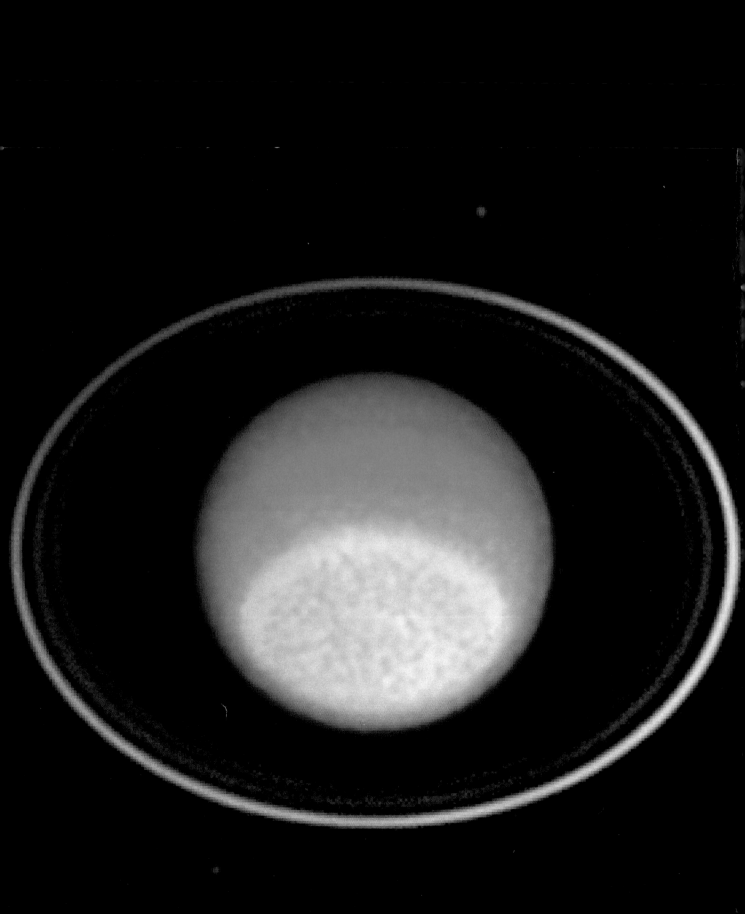

The Rings of Uranus

In 1977, Uranus passed in front of a star. The only place to view this event was over the Indian Ocean. A group of astronomers took a plane above the ocean. They pointed a large telescope at Uranus. Astronomers wanted to discover more about the planet's atmosphere.

The star's light passed through Uranus's atmosphere as the planet neared the star. Astronomers watched how the star's light changed. Astronomers saw something they did not expect to happen.

When Uranus was close to the star, the star's light blinked off and on five times. After Uranus passed in front of the star, the star blinked off and on five more times. The astronomers discovered five rings that circle Uranus. The star appeared to blink as the rings moved in front of the star.

The Hubble Space Telescope took this picture of Uranus and its rings.

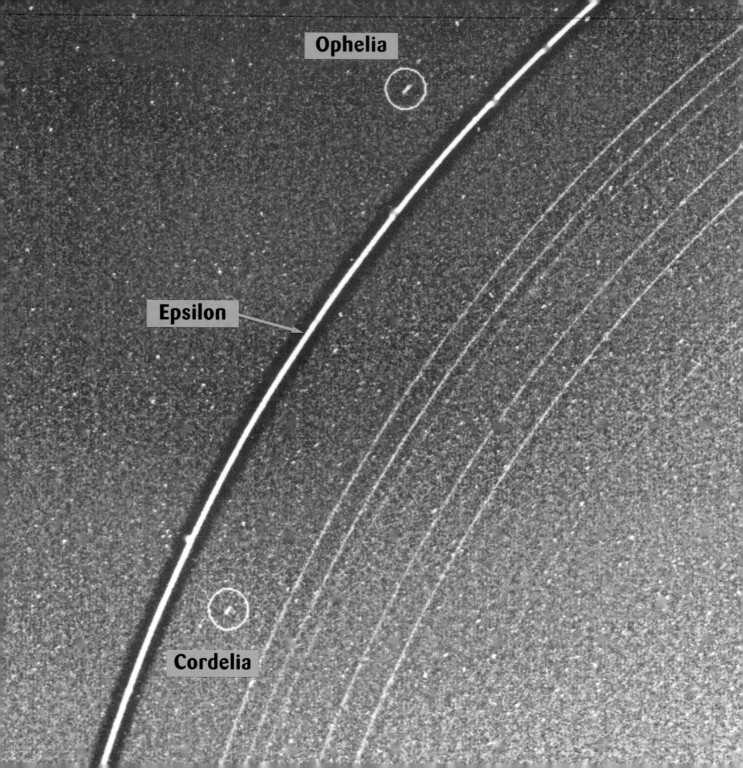

More Rings Found

Since 1977, scientists have discovered six more rings that circle Uranus. In all, astronomers have found 11 rings that circle the planet.

Uranus's rings are hard to see because they are very dark. They are made of dust and rocks. Not all the rings circle the entire planet. Some rings have gaps.

The outer ring, called Epsilon, is the brightest of the rings. This gray ring is made of ice boulders.

Uranus has two small moons that affect Epsilon. The moons Cordelia and Ophelia travel near this outer ring. The gravity from the moons keeps the boulders in the ring together. Astronomers call Cordelia and Ophelia shepherd moons.

Astronomers think Uranus's rings were made at different times. They believe some of the rings formed when meteorites crashed into a moon.

Cordelia and Ophelia travel near the ring Epsilon.

Uranus has at least 18 moons. Five large moons and at least 13 small moons orbit Uranus. All the moons are less than 1,000 miles (1,600 kilometers) wide.

The 13 small moons are each less than 100 miles (160 kilometers) wide. Cordelia, the smallest moon, is only 16 miles (26 kilometers) wide. Cordelia is Uranus's closest moon. Cordelia orbits the planet at a distance of 30,914 miles (49,750 kilometers).

Astronomers are not sure how many small moons Uranus has. They continue to discover more of Uranus's small moons. In 1999, they discovered evidence of three more small moons. Uranus might have as many as 21 moons.

Astronomers think more small moons may travel through Uranus's ring system. They have not yet found these moons.

The space probe *Voyager 2* took this picture of Uranus's rings. The Hubble Space Telescope took the smaller picture of Uranus's rings and some of its small moons.

Titania

Oberon

Miranda

Umbriel

Ariel

Large Moons

Uranus's five large moons are made of rock and ice. These moons are very cold. All five moons are dark gray and have giant cracks like those caused by earthquakes on Earth.

The largest moon is Titania. This moon is 982 miles (1,580 kilometers) wide. Moving ice probably created Titania's huge cracks and canyons.

Oberon is the next largest moon. Many meteorites have crashed into Oberon. Craters cover this moon's surface.

Umbriel has unusually large craters. This moon has a mark that looks like a giant doughnut.

Ariel's surface appears similar to Titania's. Ariel has huge valleys that criss-cross its surface.

Miranda looks different from the other large moons. Miranda looks like something smashed it into big pieces. But the pieces somehow stayed together. One feature on Miranda's surface looks like a giant check mark.

The *Voyager 2* space probe took these pictures of Uranus's five largest moons.

Exploring Uranus

People knew very little about Uranus before 1977. The planet was too far away to study easily. Astronomers knew about five of the planet's moons, its distance from Earth, and the size of its orbit.

In 1977, astronomers discovered Uranus's ring system. They sent the *Voyager 2* space probe to the outer planets in 1977. This spacecraft flew by Uranus in 1986.

Voyager 2 gave astronomers their first close-up pictures of Uranus. They discovered new rings and 10 more moons. Since 1986, astronomers have discovered at least three more of Uranus's moons.

Scientists will not send another space probe to Uranus for many years. Sending a space probe to this faraway planet is expensive.

The *Voyager 2* space probe flew by Uranus in January 1986.

Hands On: Discovering Rings

Astronomers discovered Uranus's rings in 1977 when the planet crossed in front of a star. You can see how they made this discovery. You should do this activity at night.

What You Need

Styrofoam ball
Large nail
Pipe cleaner
Streetlight

What You Do

1. Push the point of the nail into the ball.
2. Wrap one end of the pipe cleaner around the nail. Wrap the pipe cleaner in a large circle around the ball. The pipe cleaner should not touch the ball. Bring the free end of the pipe cleaner back to the nail and wrap it around the nail.
3. The ball represents Uranus. The pipe cleaner is one of its rings.
4. Turn off the lights. Look out the window in the direction of a streetlight.
5. Hold the model you made by the nail. Slowly pass the model between the light and your eye.

When Uranus passed in front of the star, astronomers saw the star's light blink. This meant that Uranus has rings.

Words to Know

atmosphere (AT-muhss-feehr)—a mixture of gases that surrounds some planets

gravity (GRAV-uh-tee)—a force that pulls objects together

meteorite (MEE-tee-ur-rite)—a piece of space rock that strikes a planet or a moon

orbit (OR-bit)—the path of an object as it travels around another object in space

revolution (rev-uh-LOO-shuhn)—the movement of one object around another object in space

ring (RING)—a band of rock and dust orbiting a planet

rotation (roh-TAY-shuhn)—one complete spin of an object in space

space probe (SPAYSS PROHB)—a spacecraft that travels to other planets and outer space

telescope (TEL-uh-skope)—an instrument that makes faraway objects seem larger and closer

Read More

Brimner, Larry Dane. *Uranus*. A True Book. New York: Children's Press, 1999.

Kerrod, Robin. *Astronomy*. Young Scientist Concepts and Projects. Milwaukee: Gareth Stevens, 1998.

Kerrod, Robin. *Uranus, Neptune, and Pluto*. Planet Library. Minneapolis: Lerner, 2000.

Useful Addresses

Canadian Space Agency
6767 Route de l'Aéroport
Saint-Hubert, QC J3Y 8Y9
Canada

NASA Headquarters
Washington, DC 20546-0001

The Planetary Society
65 Catalina Avenue
Pasadena, CA 91106-2301

Internet Sites

The Nine Planets
http://www.tcsn.net/afiner
The Space Place
http://spaceplace.jpl.nasa.gov/spacepl.htm
StarChild
http://starchild.gsfc.nasa.gov/docs/StarChild/
    StarChild.html

Index